Motivational! Cha

Powerful! Strictly Business!

MINDING MY OWN BUSINESS

A Guide for Managing and Stabilizing My Personal Budget, GOD's Way

L. A. Smith

GOD'S LITTLE MESSENGER

New Edition, 2008
Copyright © 2002; 2008 by L. A. Smith Roberts. All Rights Reserved.

ISBN: 9781403362506

No part of this book may be reproduced, stored in a retrieval system, or transmitted by any means, electronic, mechanical, photocopying, recording, or otherwise, without written permission from the author.

GNGA Publishing Division
Good News & Give Aways, Inc.
P.O. Box 929
Gainesville, VA 20156

Email: Goodnews23@aol.com
LAspeaks@comcast.net

1-877-951-3474

1st Books Library (now AuthorHouse)
2595 Vernal Pike, Bloomington, IN 47404 USA, rev.11/1/02.

ISBN: 1-4033-6250-5 (Paperback)
ISBN: 1-4044-6249-1 (e-book)

PRINTED IN THE UNITED STATES OF AMERICA

PLEASE NOTE

If you have purchased this book with the **GREEN COVER**, by L.A. Smith, you have received an illegal copy. Please contact us via our website at www.LA-speaks.net or via our toll free number, 1-877-951-3474, to inquire about the updated version.

This book is available for **EDUCATIONAL USE, FUND RAISING PURPOSES**, and **BULK SALES** at a discount rate. For more details, contact GNGA, Inc., Family Budget Institute Ministry at www.LA-speaks.net; 1-877-951-3474; or by email: Goodnews23@aol.com, LAspeaks@comcast.net.

Eschelle —
You are special.
Join us in sharing God's word to help others to live a better life, His Way.
[illegible]
6-15-2010

INTRODUCTION

Matthew 6:33

"But seek first His kingdom and His righteousness and all these things will be given to you as well." **NIV**

"...and He will give you all you need from day to day if you live for Him and make the Kingdom of God your primary concern." **NLT**

Deuteronomy 8:18

"But remember the Lord your God, for it is He who gives you the ability to produce wealth, and so confirms His covenant, which He swore to your forefathers, as it is today." **NIV**

"Always remember that it is the Lord your God who gives you power to become rich, and He does it to fulfill the covenant He made with your ancestors." **NLT**

I Thessalonians 4:11

"Make it your ambition to lead a quiet life, to mind your own business and to work with your hands, just as we told you,..." **NIV**

"This should be your ambition: to live a quiet life, minding your own business and working with your hands, just as we commanded you before." **NLT**

Kids will be kids. Don't you remember when you wanted something so bad that you could almost taste it or feel it? Of course, it happened to you as it did the rest of us. It happened to me as an adult, more than once; but sharing this one significant time is necessary so that you will learn how and why I ultimately accepted my Divine calling into the ministry as a teaching evangelist.

BUT SEEK FIRST HIS KINGDOM... Following my divorce, my college graduation, buying my first home and raising my one and only child, better than most two parent families, I asked God to allow me to have my own business. HE DID. After about seven years as the owner/manager of a print shop and an insurance agency, I prayed to be delivered from this dreadful, overwhelming dream. You know the story, I was working long hours and paying everybody, except myself. "I want out, Lord! Help me!" is what I cried. After dealing with an unscrupulous attorney who made matters worse for me, I finally found the 'real me' again after about five years of managing obligatory debt caused by others. This was a very challenging life experience that taught me how to help many people with financial problems.

ALWAYS REMEMBER THAT IT IS THE LORD YOUR GOD WHO GIVES YOU POWER... First of all, I did not ever want to be a teacher. I did not feel that I had what it takes to be as great as some of the instructors that I had when I was growing up. I will always remember the ones who seemed to be so demanding and tough. Yet, I learned more from them because they expected more from me. Well, it is the same way with God, the *greatest teacher of all*. His manner of training His children is inexplicably superior and unforgettable.

After you have rebelled, refused, denied and hidden from your true calling you are, at some point, forced to realize that you have to make a choice to live for him in peace or to live a life of misery. I was miserable for several years because I suffered from all of the above anxieties. The bottom line was fear of rejection from people whom I tried to help. They asked for my assistance and yet, some of them refused to follow the plan that God had given me for them. When they later learned from other sources that they had missed a great opportunity, they wanted to know why I didn't make them listen. GIVE ME A BREAK! So, I decided to relocate; rather, to run away. Having more work than I could handle but very few dollars was beginning to put too much weight on my shoulders. Most of my budget clients did not have money or very much to donate for my services.

In addition, criticism from family members was constant. I was told, "You have all that education, but nothing else." The person was referring to material possessions. God did not seem to listen to my prayers. I knew He heard me, but He was waiting on me to do it His way.

So, I accepted a position in a southern part of Georgia. I did not know anyone there. In fact, I could not find the town on the map. After almost a year and a few thousand dollars from savings and investments, I moved from there to the Atlanta area. Certainly, I will make money here and live a good semi-retired life in this big metropolis, I thought. I was so wrong. The same situation repeated itself. There were so many people who were losing their homes to foreclosure and/or they owed three times more than their incomes. Thus, I had plenty of work, but no money. I served on various boards and people loved my ideas, but not enough to extend a contract.

Two years later as I was driving home from an appointment that I almost didn't keep, I found myself literally crying to the Lord that He was all I had. I needed His help because I didn't know anything else to do. Then, I reflected on how He had provided for me on this particular appointment. I had prayed for direction because I had enough money to buy food and return home or to buy gasoline for my car and go to the appointment. By now you should know what I was thinking...this was probably another pitiful case and the prospective client would not have the initial donation for me to begin to work on her situation. Well, thank God I listened and I was happily surprised. The lady gave her donation in cash and had collected all the documentation for me to help her. You see, when you walk in the path that He has designed for you, He gives you a little sunshine when you think it's gloomy. That is the Lord's way of letting you know that He is in total control.

MAKE IT YOUR AMBITION TO LEAD A QUIET LIFE, TO MIND YOUR OWN BUSINESS...

I had a serious discussion (prayer) with God during a time when I sat in my favorite chair and realized that I did NOT like my life. I was so unhappy, broke and existing in a daily daze that left me feeling worse each day. I made an agreement with the Lord. I actually told Him that I would continue to do this ministry with eagerness if He would take care of me and help me to follow His direction. I was so tired of living in a downward position.

YES; I continued to assist people whether or not they had money. Somehow I was receiving more benefits. There were a few clients who did not have a debt situation, but they needed budgeting and investment knowledge. They donated fees that compensated for others.

After additional training and certifications, I applied and was accepted as a member of a national Vocational Evangelist Conference. I had met all the necessary requirements based on years of unofficially working in the ministry. Remember the sunshine that God gives? He gave me a partner in marriage and in my work. God worked another miracle by allowing me to receive an invitation and the approval to go to Amsterdam in the year 2000. God and I were not listed in the printed program to teach, but we seized the opportunity when there was a vacancy. Instructing the seventy plus conferees (pastors and church leaders from various countries) has enhanced our ministry's growth. We built our own debt free structure, known to people who come for training as the Family Budget Institute. For two years, we devoted much time to a weekly radio broadcast. We now conduct four to five major conferences or retreats each year for individuals and families with children. MAKE GOD SMILE. Use this book to improve your life and BECOME A WINNER!

L. A. Smith, Author

DEDICATION

To my best friend, my Mother
MRS. ROSE TUCKER HICKS

To my God-given Partner,
EDWARD ROBERTS

And to my beloved Son,
TONY A. SMITH

FOREWORD

By Rev. Dr. I. Benni Singleton

GOD has bestowed upon L. A. Smith, a number of gifts. She is a *writer,* a *speaker* and a *singer.* She is a very talented soprano. L. A. also has been gifted with the capacity to understand money management and has chosen as her ministry to accede to God's calling to go TEACH and HELP others with their finances.

We are all affected and effected by the financial aspects of our lives, whether we are rich, middle income or poor. In this writing, L. A. Smith offers a very practical and realistic approach to looking at the economic formula that influences and impacts upon our day-to-day living.

Evangelist Smith goes beyond those separate entities of possessions and seques into the influence and confluence of God's expectations upon our daily living. L. A. is not only a financial wizard with a special spiritual calling to serve, but she is a spiritual person—a Christian person.

L. A. Smith's ***"MINDING MY OWN BUSINESS"*** is a manual for financial and spiritual living that is not only a meaningful, instructive and advisory reading, but a practical guide to goals spiritually interwoven. It defines the religious implications and spiritual impact upon our income, outflow and checks and balances.

THIS IS A CLINICAL MANUAL OF FINANCE THAT SHOULD BE IN EVERYBODY'S RESOURCE LIBRARY.

I. Benni Singleton, Interim Pastor
Pennsylvania Avenue Baptist Church
Washington, D. C.

TABLE OF CONTENTS

The FIRST Chapter

MY CREDIT and DEBT STATUS

I am convinced that most people do not know what is meant by *'credit status' and/or 'debt status.'* To briefly explain, let's look at where I am now with my output of money and whether or not the business world regards me as *'credit worthy.'* The best view of this picture is to create a record or list of all debts or installment payments.

I will complete the information required on the form by getting the most recent statement or invoice from my creditors and writing this data in its proper place.

INSTALLMENT DEBT WORKSHEET
(Major Loans, Credit/Charge Cards, Short Term & Personal Loans)

Month ________ **Year** ________

Account Name	Credit Limit	Balance Owed	Interest Rate	Monthly Payment
Mortgage _____	$ ________	$ ________	________ %	$ ________
Auto Loan _____	________	________	________	________
Auto Loan _____	________	________	________	________
SubTotals	**$** ________	**$** ________	________ **%**	**$** ________
________	$ ________	$ ________	________ %	$ ________
________	________	________	________	________
________	________	________	________	________
________	________	________	________	________
________	________	________	________	________
SubTotals	**$** ________	**$** ________	________ **%**	**$** ________
TOTALS	**$** ________	**$** ________	________ **%**	**$** ________

IMPORTANT REMINDERS

Personal debts that I may owe to a family member or a friend will not have a credit limit but the amount that is listed on the worksheet is the *original sum* that was borrowed. In most instances, there is no interest or percentage rate involved.

If I do not have a current (less than four months old) credit report, I will telephone or write to one or two of the three major credit repositories to obtain my record. Upon receipt, I will check for accuracy and concurrence with my installment worksheet. I will also review the credit rating that is listed for each debt that appears. If married or divorced within a three year period, I will look at the type of account that is recorded to determine if I have been erroneously included for debt that had been acquired by my present or former spouse.

MAJOR CREDIT REPOSITORIES

EQUIFAX
Equifax Credit Information Services
P. O. Box 740123
Atlanta, GA 30374
1 (800) 685-1111

TRANS UNION
TransUnion Marketing Opt-Out
P. O. Box 97328
Jackson, MS 39288
1 (800) 916-8800

EXPERIAN
(formerly TRW)
P. O. Box 919
Allen, TX 75013
1 (800) 682-7654

While reviewing my credit report, I will check for collections, judgments and any other negative transactions that might appear. It may be a good idea to have my overall credit score included when I request my credit record. All this information will allow me to have a clearer, detailed status of my debt and credit history. When you KNOW WHERE YOU ARE, you are in a better position to determine how to GET TO WHERE YOU WANT TO BE. The real work truly begins as I continue.

DEBT FREE and/or MANAGING MONTHLY HOUSEHOLD EXPENSES?

Continue reading and writing your own plan.

IN DEBT?

You should seriously read this book and develop your personal budget and financial goals.

PERSEVERANCE

"Patient endurance is what you need now, so you will continue to do God's will. Then you will receive all that He has promised."...NLT Hebrews 10:36

The SECOND Chapter

MY PERSONAL (INDIVIDUAL/FAMILY) GOALS

Some people feel that they do not accomplish very much because there is not enough time during a given day. Believe me, I know this is more of a myth than fact. There are twenty-four hours in a day which equals 168 hours in a week. That is a lot of time when it is properly utilized. I am learning that we must stop procrastinating and make a list of concerns or ideas that need to be accomplished. After making this list, I carefully examine all the items and put a priority (number) next to each one so that I will know which one to do first, second and so forth. Sometimes I rewrite this list in the new order. This gives me a plan or a sense of direction for the day or perhaps for the week. Two sample forms or charts for developing this plan are below. Select your choice.

THINGS *'TO DO'* LIST

Priority #	Item	Date	Done	Incomplete
____	______________________	______	______	________
____	______________________	______	______	________
____	______________________	______	______	________
____	______________________	______	______	________
____	______________________	______	______	________
____	______________________	______	______	________
____	______________________	______	______	________
____	______________________	______	______	________
____	______________________	______	______	________
____	______________________	______	______	________

WEEKLY or MONTHLY LIST

	WK 1	WK 2	WK 3	WK 4
Sunday				
Monday				
Tuesday				
Wednesday				
Thursday				
Friday				
Saturday				

There are many people who have been taught to work hard. Yet, I have learned that it is *not* how hard you work but how *smart.* We must have a plan and preferably a written one. The Holy Scriptures teach us that God has plans for us. Research Genesis, Chapters 43, 45; Matthew, Chapters 1, 2,

27 and lastly, Ephesians, Chapters 1 and 3. There are many other books that can provide insight about God's many plans and His overall plan for each of us. Think about it!

Why do we need road maps or why do builders need architectural drawings?

As I consider the work that I have completed on the charts to this point, I feel I am about to embark on the most important and difficult segment in this process. Some individuals find it challenging to write or verbalize a clear goal.

For instance: **My goal is to find peace and happiness within the next year with my finances.** Sorry; this is NOT a goal, but a wish in its abstract form. To formulate this desire into an attainable accomplishment, I have to ask myself these questions. 1) Is the statement realistic and/or tangible? 2) Can various steps be derived toward making this idea into a completed reality?

Example of a good goal: **Within twelve months, I will develop a budget and payment structure that will allow me to take control of my financial situation.**

This statement is expressing these procedures: a) Development of a budget and payment plan; and b) Management of my financial situation within twelve months (which will add peace of mind). The following chart will help me to see my goals in written form.

PLAN; DON'T WORRY!

***"...Careful planning is thinking ahead about goals, steps and schedules and trusting God's guidance. Worriers who worry about tomorrow allow their plans to interfere with their relationship with God."...*NLT Matthew 6:34 (Life Application Notes)**

MY (OUR) GOALS
WISH—→ GOAL = A REALISTIC ACCOMPLISHMENT
The Miracle Process

SHORT TERM (Less than 12 months) **Start Date** ______________
(PRAY for Direction and Assistance.)

My **WISH** is ____

My **GOAL** (based on the above wish) is ______________________________

ACTION STEPS (What I Need To Do) NOTE: Number of procedures may vary.

A. ______________________________ Due Date __________
B. ______________________________ Due Date __________
C. ______________________________ Due Date __________

INTERMEDIATE (One Year, but Less than Five) **Start Date** ______________
(PRAY for Direction and Assistance.)

My **WISH** is ____

My **GOAL** (based on the above wish) is ______________________________

ACTION STEPS (What I Need To Do) NOTE: Number of procedures may vary.

A. ______________________________ Due Date __________
B. ______________________________ Due Date __________
C. ______________________________ Due Date __________

LONG TERM (Five years or Longer) **Start Date** ______________
(PRAY for Direction and Assistance.)

My **WISH** is ____

My **GOAL** (based on the above wish) is ______________________________

ACTION STEPS (What I Need To Do) NOTE: Number of procedures may vary.

A. ______________________________ Due Date __________
B. ______________________________ Due Date __________
C. ______________________________ Due Date __________

The THIRD Chapter

MY 13 MONTHS' BUDGET

(Including My Daily Log)

As a brief, but necessary reminder, I must acknowledge that everything I have in my possession does not belong to me. Everything that I have accomplished, whether tangible or intangible, is not mine. IT ALL BELONGS TO GOD! But, God has entrusted me to manage ALL these things. Therefore, as a good steward or trustee, I am striving to utilize these resources with the abilities that He has given me. The skillful level at which I do this job will determine the accomplishments that I will add to expanding God's Kingdom.

The proper management of what one has, regardless of how small or how large, is the key to gaining *more to manage*. Many people who are struggling from paycheck to paycheck sometimes utter, "All I need is a little more money." The fact is, all one needs is a little more knowledge that can be applied to a 'workable' plan. This plan in simple terms is the budget. Assuming that big corporations have more money and assets than average working individuals or families, why do you suppose they operate from carefully planned financial statements and projections of estimated expenditures and revenues?

In the following pages, I will study and create a budget each month for thirteen months. These monthly cash flow worksheets will start with December and end with December of the next year. My rationale for the thirteen month concept is based on closing out one calendar year and simultaneously, planning for the next one. When the first day of the new year arrives, the budget for that month should already be formulated. Remember; procrastination could hinder and destroy me. My goal is, not to lose what God has given me, but to increase my overall growth for His sake.

MONTHLY CASH FLOW WORKSHEET December, 20_______

INCOME SOURCES	(Total All MONTHLY Net or 'Take Home' Amounts.)
SALARY (from current PRIMARY employment)	$ ____________
PART TIME JOB Earnings	____________
SOCIAL SECURITY/PENSION	____________
CHILD SUPPORT INCOME/ALIMOMY INCOME	____________
TRUST FUND INCOME	____________
RENTAL INCOME	____________
STOCK/BOND PROCEEDS	____________
MISCELLANEOUS INCOME	____________
TOTAL MONTHLY INCOME	**$ ____________**

FIXED (Stationary) **EXPENDITURES**	**Current Amount Due**	**Actual Payment**
MORTGAGE/RENT	$ ________	$ ________
FUEL (Heating Oil, Gas, Electricity)	________	________
ELECTRICITY (No Heating)	________	________
WATER/SEWAGE	________	________
TELEPHONE	________	________
PERS. PROPERTY TAXES	________	________
AUTO LOAN, #1	________	________
AUTO LOAN, #2	________	________
AUTO INSURANCE PREMIUM	________	________
LIFE INSURANCE PREMIUM	________	________
MEDICAL/DISABILITY INSURANCE PREM.	________	________
HOMEOWNER'S INSURANCE PREMIUM	________	________
CREDIT CARD ____________	________	________
CREDIT CARD ____________	________	________
OTHER INSTALLMENT PAYMENTS	________	________
TOTAL FIXED EXPENSES	**$ ________**	**$ ________**
FLEXIBLE (Changeable) **EXPENDITURES**		
DONATIONS, TITHES, OFFERINGS	$ ________	$ ________
GROCERIES/BEVERAGES	________	________
BEAUTICIAN, BARBER, COSMETICS, etc.	________	________
CLOTHING	________	________
LAUNDRY/CLEANING	________	________
GASOLINE/AUTO MAINTENANCE	________	________
COMMUTE (Bus, Subway, Taxi, etc.)	________	________
ENTERTAINMENT (Restaurants, Theater, etc.)	________	________
TRAVEL/VACATION	________	________
MEDICAL COPAYS/PRESCRIPTIONS	________	________
CHILD CARE	________	________
INVESTMENTS/SAVINGS	________	________
PERSONAL ALLOWANCE	________	________
MISCELLANEOUS	________	________
TOTAL FLEXIBLE EXPENSES	**$ ________**	**$ ________**
COMBINED TOTAL EXPENDITURES	**$ ________**	**$ ________**

MY DAILY LOG OF GRACE

I will write any significant comment that involves ME on each day. At six months' intervals, I will review this entire month to discover my spiritual and financial growth experiences.

DEC., 20 ______ DAILY ENTRY * BENEFIT * BLESSING

DAY 1 ______
2 ______
3 ______
4 ______
5 ______
6 ______
7 ______

8 ______
9 ______
10 ______
11 ______
12 ______
13 ______
14 ______

15 ______
16 ______
17 ______
18 ______
19 ______
20 ______
21 ______

22 ______
23 ______
24 ______
25 ______
26 ______
27 ______

28 ______
29 ______
30 ______
31 ______

MONTHLY CASH FLOW WORKSHEET January, 20______

INCOME SOURCES (Total All MONTHLY Net or 'Take Home' Amounts.)

SALARY (from current PRIMARY employment)	$ ________
PART TIME JOB Earnings	________
SOCIAL SECURITY/PENSION	________
CHILD SUPPORT INCOME/ALIMOMY INCOME	________
TRUST FUND INCOME	________
RENTAL INCOME	________
STOCK/BOND PROCEEDS	________
MISCELLANEOUS INCOME	________
TOTAL MONTHLY INCOME	**$ ________**

FIXED (Stationary) **EXPENDITURES**	**Current Amount Due**	**Actual Payment**
MORTGAGE/RENT	$ ________	$ ________
FUEL (Heating Oil, Gas, Electricity)	________	________
ELECTRICITY (No Heating)	________	________
WATER/SEWAGE	________	________
TELEPHONE	________	________
PERS. PROPERTY TAXES	________	________
AUTO LOAN, #1	________	________
AUTO LOAN, #2	________	________
AUTO INSURANCE PREMIUM	________	________
LIFE INSURANCE PREMIUM	________	________
MEDICAL/DISABILITY INSURANCE PREM.	________	________
HOMEOWNER'S INSURANCE PREMIUM	________	________
CREDIT CARD ________	________	________
CREDIT CARD ________	________	________
OTHER INSTALLMENT PAYMENTS	________	________
TOTAL FIXED EXPENSES	**$ ________**	**$ ________**
FLEXIBLE (Changeable) **EXPENDITURES**		
DONATIONS, TITHES, OFFERINGS	$ ________	$ ________
GROCERIES/BEVERAGES	________	________
BEAUTICIAN, BARBER, COSMETICS, etc.	________	________
CLOTHING	________	________
LAUNDRY/CLEANING	________	________
GASOLINE/AUTO MAINTENANCE	________	________
COMMUTE (Bus, Subway, Taxi, etc.)	________	________
ENTERTAINMENT (Restaurants, Theater, etc.)	________	________
TRAVEL/VACATION	________	________
MEDICAL COPAYS/PRESCRIPTIONS	________	________
CHILD CARE	________	________
INVESTMENTS/SAVINGS	________	________
PERSONAL ALLOWANCE	________	________
MISCELLANEOUS	________	________
TOTAL FLEXIBLE EXPENSES	**$ ________**	**$ ________**
COMBINED TOTAL EXPENDITURES	**$ ________**	**$ ________**

MY DAILY LOG OF GRACE

I will write any significant comment that involves ME on each day. At six months' intervals, I will review this entire month to discover my spiritual and financial growth experiences.

JAN.,20 ______ **DAILY ENTRY * BENEFIT * BLESSING**

DAY 1 ______________________________
2 ______________________________
3 ______________________________
4 ______________________________
5 ______________________________
6 ______________________________
7 ______________________________

8 ______________________________
9 ______________________________
10 ______________________________
11 ______________________________
12 ______________________________
13 ______________________________
14 ______________________________

15 ______________________________
16 ______________________________
17 ______________________________
18 ______________________________
19 ______________________________
20 ______________________________
21 ______________________________

22 ______________________________
23 ______________________________
24 ______________________________
25 ______________________________
26 ______________________________
27 ______________________________

28 ______________________________
29 ______________________________
30 ______________________________
31 ______________________________

MONTHLY CASH FLOW WORKSHEET February, 20______

INCOME SOURCES (Total All MONTHLY Net or 'Take Home' Amounts.)

SALARY (from current PRIMARY employment)	$ ________
PART TIME JOB Earnings	________
SOCIAL SECURITY/PENSION	________
CHILD SUPPORT INCOME/ALIMOMY INCOME	________
TRUST FUND INCOME	________
RENTAL INCOME	________
STOCK/BOND PROCEEDS	________
MISCELLANEOUS INCOME	________
TOTAL MONTHLY INCOME	**$ ________**

FIXED (Stationary) EXPENDITURES	**Current Amount Due**	**Actual Payment**
MORTGAGE/RENT	$ ________	$ ________
FUEL (Heating Oil, Gas, Electricity)	________	________
ELECTRICITY (No Heating)	________	________
WATER/SEWAGE	________	________
TELEPHONE	________	________
PERS. PROPERTY TAXES	________	________
AUTO LOAN, #1	________	________
AUTO LOAN, #2	________	________
AUTO INSURANCE PREMIUM	________	________
LIFE INSURANCE PREMIUM	________	________
MEDICAL/DISABILITY INSURANCE PREM.	________	________
HOMEOWNER'S INSURANCE PREMIUM	________	________
CREDIT CARD ________	________	________
CREDIT CARD ________	________	________
OTHER INSTALLMENT PAYMENTS	________	________
TOTAL FIXED EXPENSES	**$ ________**	**$ ________**
FLEXIBLE (Changeable) EXPENDITURES		
DONATIONS, TITHES, OFFERINGS	$ ________	$ ________
GROCERIES/BEVERAGES	________	________
BEAUTICIAN, BARBER, COSMETICS, etc.	________	________
CLOTHING	________	________
LAUNDRY/CLEANING	________	________
GASOLINE/AUTO MAINTENANCE	________	________
COMMUTE (Bus, Subway, Taxi, etc.)	________	________
ENTERTAINMENT (Restaurants, Theater, etc.)	________	________
TRAVEL/VACATION	________	________
MEDICAL COPAYS/PRESCRIPTIONS	________	________
CHILD CARE	________	________
INVESTMENTS/SAVINGS	________	________
PERSONAL ALLOWANCE	________	________
MISCELLANEOUS	________	________
TOTAL FLEXIBLE EXPENSES	**$ ________**	**$ ________**
COMBINED TOTAL EXPENDITURES	**$ ________**	**$ ________**

MY DAILY LOG OF GRACE

I will write any significant comment that involves ME on each day. At six months' intervals, I will review this entire month to discover my spiritual and financial growth experiences.

FEB.,20 ______ **DAILY ENTRY * BENEFIT * BLESSING**

DAY 1 ____________________
2 ____________________
3 ____________________
4 ____________________
5 ____________________
6 ____________________
7 ____________________

8 ____________________
9 ____________________
10 ____________________
11 ____________________
12 ____________________
13 ____________________
14 ____________________

15 ____________________
16 ____________________
17 ____________________
18 ____________________
19 ____________________
20 ____________________
21 ____________________

22 ____________________
23 ____________________
24 ____________________
25 ____________________
26 ____________________
27 ____________________

28 ____________________
29 ____________________
30 ____________________
31 ____________________

MONTHLY CASH FLOW WORKSHEET March, 20______

INCOME SOURCES	(Total All MONTHLY Net or 'Take Home' Amounts.)
SALARY (from current PRIMARY employment)	$ ______________
PART TIME JOB Earnings	______________
SOCIAL SECURITY/PENSION	______________
CHILD SUPPORT INCOME/ALIMOMY INCOME	______________
TRUST FUND INCOME	______________
RENTAL INCOME	______________
STOCK/BOND PROCEEDS	______________
MISCELLANEOUS INCOME	______________
TOTAL MONTHLY INCOME	$ ______________

FIXED (Stationary) **EXPENDITURES**	**Current Amount Due**	**Actual Payment**
MORTGAGE/RENT	$ __________	$ __________
FUEL (Heating Oil, Gas, Electricity)	__________	__________
ELECTRICITY (No Heating)	__________	__________
WATER/SEWAGE	__________	__________
TELEPHONE	__________	__________
PERS. PROPERTY TAXES	__________	__________
AUTO LOAN, #1	__________	__________
AUTO LOAN, #2	__________	__________
AUTO INSURANCE PREMIUM	__________	__________
LIFE INSURANCE PREMIUM	__________	__________
MEDICAL/DISABILITY INSURANCE PREM.	__________	__________
HOMEOWNER'S INSURANCE PREMIUM	__________	__________
CREDIT CARD ______________	__________	__________
CREDIT CARD ______________	__________	__________
OTHER INSTALLMENT PAYMENTS	__________	__________
TOTAL FIXED EXPENSES	$ __________	$ __________
FLEXIBLE (Changeable) **EXPENDITURES**		
DONATIONS, TITHES, OFFERINGS	$ __________	$ __________
GROCERIES/BEVERAGES	__________	__________
BEAUTICIAN, BARBER, COSMETICS, etc.	__________	__________
CLOTHING	__________	__________
LAUNDRY/CLEANING	__________	__________
GASOLINE/AUTO MAINTENANCE	__________	__________
COMMUTE (Bus, Subway, Taxi, etc.)	__________	__________
ENTERTAINMENT (Restaurants, Theater, etc.)	__________	__________
TRAVEL/VACATION	__________	__________
MEDICAL COPAYS/PRESCRIPTIONS	__________	__________
CHILD CARE	__________	__________
INVESTMENTS/SAVINGS	__________	__________
PERSONAL ALLOWANCE	__________	__________
MISCELLANEOUS	__________	__________
TOTAL FLEXIBLE EXPENSES	$ __________	$ __________
COMBINED TOTAL EXPENDITURES	$ __________	$ __________

MY DAILY LOG OF GRACE

I will write any significant comment that involves ME on each day. At six months' intervals, I will review this entire month to discover my spiritual and financial growth experiences.

MAR., 20______ DAILY ENTRY * BENEFIT * BLESSING

DAY 1 ____________________
2 ____________________
3 ____________________
4 ____________________
5 ____________________
6 ____________________
7 ____________________

8 ____________________
9 ____________________
10 ____________________
11 ____________________
12 ____________________
13 ____________________
14 ____________________

15 ____________________
16 ____________________
17 ____________________
18 ____________________
19 ____________________
20 ____________________
21 ____________________

22 ____________________
23 ____________________
24 ____________________
25 ____________________
26 ____________________
27 ____________________

28 ____________________
29 ____________________
30 ____________________
31 ____________________

MONTHLY CASH FLOW WORKSHEET April, 20______

INCOME SOURCES (Total All MONTHLY Net or 'Take Home' Amounts.)

SALARY (from current PRIMARY employment)	$ ____________
PART TIME JOB Earnings	____________
SOCIAL SECURITY/PENSION	____________
CHILD SUPPORT INCOME/ALIMOMY INCOME	____________
TRUST FUND INCOME	____________
RENTAL INCOME	____________
STOCK/BOND PROCEEDS	____________
MISCELLANEOUS INCOME	____________
TOTAL MONTHLY INCOME	**$ ____________**

FIXED (Stationary) **EXPENDITURES**	**Current Amount Due**	**Actual Payment**
MORTGAGE/RENT	$ ________	$ ________
FUEL (Heating Oil, Gas, Electricity)	________	________
ELECTRICITY (No Heating)	________	________
WATER/SEWAGE	________	________
TELEPHONE	________	________
PERS. PROPERTY TAXES	________	________
AUTO LOAN, #1	________	________
AUTO LOAN, #2	________	________
AUTO INSURANCE PREMIUM	________	________
LIFE INSURANCE PREMIUM	________	________
MEDICAL/DISABILITY INSURANCE PREM.	________	________
HOMEOWNER'S INSURANCE PREMIUM	________	________
CREDIT CARD ____________	________	________
CREDIT CARD ____________	________	________
OTHER INSTALLMENT PAYMENTS	________	________
TOTAL FIXED EXPENSES	**$ ________**	**$ ________**
FLEXIBLE (Changeable) **EXPENDITURES**		
DONATIONS, TITHES, OFFERINGS	$ ________	$ ________
GROCERIES/BEVERAGES	________	________
BEAUTICIAN, BARBER, COSMETICS, etc.	________	________
CLOTHING	________	________
LAUNDRY/CLEANING	________	________
GASOLINE/AUTO MAINTENANCE	________	________
COMMUTE (Bus, Subway, Taxi, etc.)	________	________
ENTERTAINMENT (Restaurants, Theater, etc.)	________	________
TRAVEL/VACATION	________	________
MEDICAL COPAYS/PRESCRIPTIONS	________	________
CHILD CARE	________	________
INVESTMENTS/SAVINGS	________	________
PERSONAL ALLOWANCE	________	________
MISCELLANEOUS	________	________
TOTAL FLEXIBLE EXPENSES	**$ ________**	**$ ________**
COMBINED TOTAL EXPENDITURES	**$ ________**	**$ ________**

MY DAILY LOG OF GRACE

I will write any significant comment that involves ME on each day. At six months' intervals, I will review this entire month to discover my spiritual and financial growth experiences.

APR.,20 ______ **DAILY ENTRY * BENEFIT * BLESSING**

DAY 1 ______
2 ______
3 ______
4 ______
5 ______
6 ______
7 ______

8 ______
9 ______
10 ______
11 ______
12 ______
13 ______
14 ______

15 ______
16 ______
17 ______
18 ______
19 ______
20 ______
21 ______

22 ______
23 ______
24 ______
25 ______
26 ______
27 ______

28 ______
29 ______
30 ______
31 ______

MONTHLY CASH FLOW WORKSHEET May, 20______

INCOME SOURCES (Total All MONTHLY Net or 'Take Home' Amounts.)

SALARY (from current PRIMARY employment)	$ ______________
PART TIME JOB Earnings	______________
SOCIAL SECURITY/PENSION	______________
CHILD SUPPORT INCOME/ALIMOMY INCOME	______________
TRUST FUND INCOME	______________
RENTAL INCOME	______________
STOCK/BOND PROCEEDS	______________
MISCELLANEOUS INCOME	______________
TOTAL MONTHLY INCOME	**$ ______________**

FIXED (Stationary) EXPENDITURES	Current Amount Due	Actual Payment
MORTGAGE/RENT	$ __________	$ __________
FUEL (Heating Oil, Gas, Electricity)	__________	__________
ELECTRICITY (No Heating)	__________	__________
WATER/SEWAGE	__________	__________
TELEPHONE	__________	__________
PERS. PROPERTY TAXES	__________	__________
AUTO LOAN, #1	__________	__________
AUTO LOAN, #2	__________	__________
AUTO INSURANCE PREMIUM	__________	__________
LIFE INSURANCE PREMIUM	__________	__________
MEDICAL/DISABILITY INSURANCE PREM.	__________	__________
HOMEOWNER'S INSURANCE PREMIUM	__________	__________
CREDIT CARD ______________	__________	__________
CREDIT CARD ______________	__________	__________
OTHER INSTALLMENT PAYMENTS	__________	__________
TOTAL FIXED EXPENSES	**$ __________**	**$ __________**

FLEXIBLE (Changeable) EXPENDITURES		
DONATIONS, TITHES, OFFERINGS	$ __________	$ __________
GROCERIES/BEVERAGES	__________	__________
BEAUTICIAN, BARBER, COSMETICS, etc.	__________	__________
CLOTHING	__________	__________
LAUNDRY/CLEANING	__________	__________
GASOLINE/AUTO MAINTENANCE	__________	__________
COMMUTE (Bus, Subway, Taxi, etc.)	__________	__________
ENTERTAINMENT (Restaurants, Theater, etc.)	__________	__________
TRAVEL/VACATION	__________	__________
MEDICAL COPAYS/PRESCRIPTIONS	__________	__________
CHILD CARE	__________	__________
INVESTMENTS/SAVINGS	__________	__________
PERSONAL ALLOWANCE	__________	__________
MISCELLANEOUS	__________	__________
TOTAL FLEXIBLE EXPENSES	**$ __________**	**$ __________**
COMBINED TOTAL EXPENDITURES	**$ __________**	**$ __________**

MY DAILY LOG OF GRACE

I will write any significant comment that involves ME on each day. At six months' intervals, I will review this entire month to discover my spiritual and financial growth experiences.

MAY,20 ______ DAILY ENTRY * BENEFIT * BLESSING

DAY 1 ____
2 ____
3 ____
4 ____
5 ____
6 ____
7 ____

8 ____
9 ____
10 ____
11 ____
12 ____
13 ____
14 ____

15 ____
16 ____
17 ____
18 ____
19 ____
20 ____
21 ____

22 ____
23 ____
24 ____
25 ____
26 ____
27 ____

28 ____
29 ____
30 ____
31 ____

MONTHLY CASH FLOW WORKSHEET June, 20______

INCOME SOURCES	(Total All MONTHLY Net or 'Take Home' Amounts.)
SALARY (from current PRIMARY employment)	$ ____________
PART TIME JOB Earnings	____________
SOCIAL SECURITY/PENSION	____________
CHILD SUPPORT INCOME/ALIMOMY INCOME	____________
TRUST FUND INCOME	____________
RENTAL INCOME	____________
STOCK/BOND PROCEEDS	____________
MISCELLANEOUS INCOME	____________
TOTAL MONTHLY INCOME	$ ____________

FIXED (Stationary) EXPENDITURES	Current Amount Due	Actual Payment
MORTGAGE/RENT	$ ________	$ ________
FUEL (Heating Oil, Gas, Electricity)	________	________
ELECTRICITY (No Heating)	________	________
WATER/SEWAGE	________	________
TELEPHONE	________	________
PERS. PROPERTY TAXES	________	________
AUTO LOAN, #1	________	________
AUTO LOAN, #2	________	________
AUTO INSURANCE PREMIUM	________	________
LIFE INSURANCE PREMIUM	________	________
MEDICAL/DISABILITY INSURANCE PREM.	________	________
HOMEOWNER'S INSURANCE PREMIUM	________	________
CREDIT CARD ____________	________	________
CREDIT CARD ____________	________	________
OTHER INSTALLMENT PAYMENTS	________	________
TOTAL FIXED EXPENSES	$ ________	$ ________
FLEXIBLE (Changeable) EXPENDITURES		
DONATIONS, TITHES, OFFERINGS	$ ________	$ ________
GROCERIES/BEVERAGES	________	________
BEAUTICIAN, BARBER, COSMETICS, etc.	________	________
CLOTHING	________	________
LAUNDRY/CLEANING	________	________
GASOLINE/AUTO MAINTENANCE	________	________
COMMUTE (Bus, Subway, Taxi, etc.)	________	________
ENTERTAINMENT (Restaurants, Theater, etc.)	________	________
TRAVEL/VACATION	________	________
MEDICAL COPAYS/PRESCRIPTIONS	________	________
CHILD CARE	________	________
INVESTMENTS/SAVINGS	________	________
PERSONAL ALLOWANCE	________	________
MISCELLANEOUS	________	________
TOTAL FLEXIBLE EXPENSES	$ ________	$ ________
COMBINED TOTAL EXPENDITURES	$ ________	$ ________

MY DAILY LOG OF GRACE

I will write any significant comment that involves ME on each day. At six months' intervals, I will review this entire month to discover my spiritual and financial growth experiences.

JUN., 20______ **DAILY ENTRY * BENEFIT * BLESSING**

DAY 1 ________________
2 ________________
3 ________________
4 ________________
5 ________________
6 ________________
7 ________________

8 ________________
9 ________________
10 ________________
11 ________________
12 ________________
13 ________________
14 ________________

15 ________________
16 ________________
17 ________________
18 ________________
19 ________________
20 ________________
21 ________________

22 ________________
23 ________________
24 ________________
25 ________________
26 ________________
27 ________________

28 ________________
29 ________________
30 ________________
31 ________________

MONTHLY CASH FLOW WORKSHEET July, 20______

INCOME SOURCES (Total All MONTHLY Net or 'Take Home' Amounts.)

SALARY (from current PRIMARY employment)	$ ____________
PART TIME JOB Earnings	____________
SOCIAL SECURITY/PENSION	____________
CHILD SUPPORT INCOME/ALIMOMY INCOME	____________
TRUST FUND INCOME	____________
RENTAL INCOME	____________
STOCK/BOND PROCEEDS	____________
MISCELLANEOUS INCOME	____________
TOTAL MONTHLY INCOME	**$ ____________**

FIXED (Stationary) EXPENDITURES	Current Amount Due	Actual Payment
MORTGAGE/RENT	$ ________	$ ________
FUEL (Heating Oil, Gas, Electricity)	________	________
ELECTRICITY (No Heating)	________	________
WATER/SEWAGE	________	________
TELEPHONE	________	________
PERS. PROPERTY TAXES	________	________
AUTO LOAN, #1	________	________
AUTO LOAN, #2	________	________
AUTO INSURANCE PREMIUM	________	________
LIFE INSURANCE PREMIUM	________	________
MEDICAL/DISABILITY INSURANCE PREM.	________	________
HOMEOWNER'S INSURANCE PREMIUM	________	________
CREDIT CARD ____________	________	________
CREDIT CARD ____________	________	________
OTHER INSTALLMENT PAYMENTS	________	________
TOTAL FIXED EXPENSES	**$ ________**	**$ ________**
FLEXIBLE (Changeable) EXPENDITURES		
DONATIONS, TITHES, OFFERINGS	$ ________	$ ________
GROCERIES/BEVERAGES	________	________
BEAUTICIAN, BARBER, COSMETICS, etc.	________	________
CLOTHING	________	________
LAUNDRY/CLEANING	________	________
GASOLINE/AUTO MAINTENANCE	________	________
COMMUTE (Bus, Subway, Taxi, etc.)	________	________
ENTERTAINMENT (Restaurants, Theater, etc.)	________	________
TRAVEL/VACATION	________	________
MEDICAL COPAYS/PRESCRIPTIONS	________	________
CHILD CARE	________	________
INVESTMENTS/SAVINGS	________	________
PERSONAL ALLOWANCE	________	________
MISCELLANEOUS	________	________
TOTAL FLEXIBLE EXPENSES	**$ ________**	**$ ________**
COMBINED TOTAL EXPENDITURES	**$ ________**	**$ ________**

MY DAILY LOG OF GRACE

I will write any significant comment that involves ME on each day. At six months' intervals, I will review this entire month to discover my spiritual and financial growth experiences.

JULY, 20______	DAILY ENTRY * BENEFIT * BLESSING
DAY 1	__________
2	__________
3	__________
4	__________
5	__________
6	__________
7	__________
8	__________
9	__________
10	__________
11	__________
12	__________
13	__________
14	__________
15	__________
16	__________
17	__________
18	__________
19	__________
20	__________
21	__________
22	__________
23	__________
24	__________
25	__________
26	__________
27	__________
28	__________
29	__________
30	__________
31	__________

MONTHLY CASH FLOW WORKSHEET August, 20______

INCOME SOURCES (Total All MONTHLY Net or 'Take Home' Amounts.)

SALARY (from current PRIMARY employment)	$ ____________
PART TIME JOB Earnings	____________
SOCIAL SECURITY/PENSION	____________
CHILD SUPPORT INCOME/ALIMOMY INCOME	____________
TRUST FUND INCOME	____________
RENTAL INCOME	____________
STOCK/BOND PROCEEDS	____________
MISCELLANEOUS INCOME	____________
TOTAL MONTHLY INCOME	**$ ____________**

FIXED (Stationary) **EXPENDITURES**	**Current Amount Due**	**Actual Payment**
MORTGAGE/RENT	$ ________	$ ________
FUEL (Heating Oil, Gas, Electricity)	________	________
ELECTRICITY (No Heating)	________	________
WATER/SEWAGE	________	________
TELEPHONE	________	________
PERS. PROPERTY TAXES	________	________
AUTO LOAN, #1	________	________
AUTO LOAN, #2	________	________
AUTO INSURANCE PREMIUM	________	________
LIFE INSURANCE PREMIUM	________	________
MEDICAL/DISABILITY INSURANCE PREM.	________	________
HOMEOWNER'S INSURANCE PREMIUM	________	________
CREDIT CARD ____________	________	________
CREDIT CARD ____________	________	________
OTHER INSTALLMENT PAYMENTS	________	________
TOTAL FIXED EXPENSES	**$ ________**	**$ ________**
FLEXIBLE (Changeable) **EXPENDITURES**		
DONATIONS, TITHES, OFFERINGS	$ ________	$ ________
GROCERIES/BEVERAGES	________	________
BEAUTICIAN, BARBER, COSMETICS, etc.	________	________
CLOTHING	________	________
LAUNDRY/CLEANING	________	________
GASOLINE/AUTO MAINTENANCE	________	________
COMMUTE (Bus, Subway, Taxi, etc.)	________	________
ENTERTAINMENT (Restaurants, Theater, etc.)	________	________
TRAVEL/VACATION	________	________
MEDICAL COPAYS/PRESCRIPTIONS	________	________
CHILD CARE	________	________
INVESTMENTS/SAVINGS	________	________
PERSONAL ALLOWANCE	________	________
MISCELLANEOUS	________	________
TOTAL FLEXIBLE EXPENSES	**$ ________**	**$ ________**
COMBINED TOTAL EXPENDITURES	**$ ________**	**$ ________**

MY DAILY LOG OF GRACE

I will write any significant comment that involves ME on each day. At six months' intervals, I will review this entire month to discover my spiritual and financial growth experiences.

AUG.,20 ______ DAILY ENTRY * BENEFIT * BLESSING

DAY 1 ____________________
2 ____________________
3 ____________________
4 ____________________
5 ____________________
6 ____________________
7 ____________________

8 ____________________
9 ____________________
10 ____________________
11 ____________________
12 ____________________
13 ____________________
14 ____________________

15 ____________________
16 ____________________
17 ____________________
18 ____________________
19 ____________________
20 ____________________
21 ____________________

22 ____________________
23 ____________________
24 ____________________
25 ____________________
26 ____________________
27 ____________________

28 ____________________
29 ____________________
30 ____________________
31 ____________________

MONTHLY CASH FLOW WORKSHEET September, 20______

INCOME SOURCES (Total All MONTHLY Net or 'Take Home' Amounts.)

SALARY (from current PRIMARY employment)	$ ____________
PART TIME JOB Earnings	____________
SOCIAL SECURITY/PENSION	____________
CHILD SUPPORT INCOME/ALIMOMY INCOME	____________
TRUST FUND INCOME	____________
RENTAL INCOME	____________
STOCK/BOND PROCEEDS	____________
MISCELLANEOUS INCOME	____________
TOTAL MONTHLY INCOME	**$ ____________**

FIXED (Stationary) **EXPENDITURES**	**Current Amount Due**	**Actual Payment**
MORTGAGE/RENT	$ ________	$ ________
FUEL (Heating Oil, Gas, Electricity)	________	________
ELECTRICITY (No Heating)	________	________
WATER/SEWAGE	________	________
TELEPHONE	________	________
PERS. PROPERTY TAXES	________	________
AUTO LOAN, #1	________	________
AUTO LOAN, #2	________	________
AUTO INSURANCE PREMIUM	________	________
LIFE INSURANCE PREMIUM	________	________
MEDICAL/DISABILITY INSURANCE PREM.	________	________
HOMEOWNER'S INSURANCE PREMIUM	________	________
CREDIT CARD ____________	________	________
CREDIT CARD ____________	________	________
OTHER INSTALLMENT PAYMENTS	________	________
TOTAL FIXED EXPENSES	**$ ________**	**$ ________**
FLEXIBLE (Changeable) **EXPENDITURES**		
DONATIONS, TITHES, OFFERINGS	$ ________	$ ________
GROCERIES/BEVERAGES	________	________
BEAUTICIAN, BARBER, COSMETICS, etc.	________	________
CLOTHING	________	________
LAUNDRY/CLEANING	________	________
GASOLINE/AUTO MAINTENANCE	________	________
COMMUTE (Bus, Subway, Taxi, etc.)	________	________
ENTERTAINMENT (Restaurants, Theater, etc.)	________	________
TRAVEL/VACATION	________	________
MEDICAL COPAYS/PRESCRIPTIONS	________	________
CHILD CARE	________	________
INVESTMENTS/SAVINGS	________	________
PERSONAL ALLOWANCE	________	________
MISCELLANEOUS	________	________
TOTAL FLEXIBLE EXPENSES	**$ ________**	**$ ________**
COMBINED TOTAL EXPENDITURES	**$ ________**	**$ ________**

MY DAILY LOG OF GRACE

I will write any significant comment that involves ME on each day. At six months' intervals, I will review this entire month to discover my spiritual and financial growth experiences.

SEP.,20_____ **DAILY ENTRY * BENEFIT * BLESSING**

DAY 1 _____
2 _____
3 _____
4 _____
5 _____
6 _____
7 _____

8 _____
9 _____
10 _____
11 _____
12 _____
13 _____
14 _____

15 _____
16 _____
17 _____
18 _____
19 _____
20 _____
21 _____

22 _____
23 _____
24 _____
25 _____
26 _____
27 _____

28 _____
29 _____
30 _____
31 _____

MONTHLY CASH FLOW WORKSHEET October, 20______

INCOME SOURCES	(Total All MONTHLY Net or 'Take Home' Amounts.)
SALARY (from current PRIMARY employment)	$ ____________
PART TIME JOB Earnings	____________
SOCIAL SECURITY/PENSION	____________
CHILD SUPPORT INCOME/ALIMOMY INCOME	____________
TRUST FUND INCOME	____________
RENTAL INCOME	____________
STOCK/BOND PROCEEDS	____________
MISCELLANEOUS INCOME	____________
TOTAL MONTHLY INCOME	**$ ____________**

FIXED (Stationary) EXPENDITURES	Current Amount Due	Actual Payment
MORTGAGE/RENT	$ ________	$ ________
FUEL (Heating Oil, Gas, Electricity)	________	________
ELECTRICITY (No Heating)	________	________
WATER/SEWAGE	________	________
TELEPHONE	________	________
PERS. PROPERTY TAXES	________	________
AUTO LOAN, #1	________	________
AUTO LOAN, #2	________	________
AUTO INSURANCE PREMIUM	________	________
LIFE INSURANCE PREMIUM	________	________
MEDICAL/DISABILITY INSURANCE PREM.	________	________
HOMEOWNER'S INSURANCE PREMIUM	________	________
CREDIT CARD ____________	________	________
CREDIT CARD ____________	________	________
OTHER INSTALLMENT PAYMENTS	________	________
TOTAL FIXED EXPENSES	**$ ________**	**$ ________**
FLEXIBLE (Changeable) EXPENDITURES		
DONATIONS, TITHES, OFFERINGS	$ ________	$ ________
GROCERIES/BEVERAGES	________	________
BEAUTICIAN, BARBER, COSMETICS, etc.	________	________
CLOTHING	________	________
LAUNDRY/CLEANING	________	________
GASOLINE/AUTO MAINTENANCE	________	________
COMMUTE (Bus, Subway, Taxi, etc.)	________	________
ENTERTAINMENT (Restaurants, Theater, etc.)	________	________
TRAVEL/VACATION	________	________
MEDICAL COPAYS/PRESCRIPTIONS	________	________
CHILD CARE	________	________
INVESTMENTS/SAVINGS	________	________
PERSONAL ALLOWANCE	________	________
MISCELLANEOUS	________	________
TOTAL FLEXIBLE EXPENSES	**$ ________**	**$ ________**
COMBINED TOTAL EXPENDITURES	**$ ________**	**$ ________**

MY DAILY LOG OF GRACE

I will write any significant comment that involves ME on each day. At six months' intervals, I will review this entire month to discover my spiritual and financial growth experiences.

OCT., 20 ______ DAILY ENTRY * BENEFIT * BLESSING

DAY 1 ______
2 ______
3 ______
4 ______
5 ______
6 ______
7 ______

8 ______
9 ______
10 ______
11 ______
12 ______
13 ______
14 ______

15 ______
16 ______
17 ______
18 ______
19 ______
20 ______
21 ______

22 ______
23 ______
24 ______
25 ______
26 ______
27 ______

28 ______
29 ______
30 ______
31 ______

MONTHLY CASH FLOW WORKSHEET November, 20______

INCOME SOURCES (Total All MONTHLY Net or 'Take Home' Amounts.)

SALARY (from current PRIMARY employment)	$ ____________
PART TIME JOB Earnings	____________
SOCIAL SECURITY/PENSION	____________
CHILD SUPPORT INCOME/ALIMOMY INCOME	____________
TRUST FUND INCOME	____________
RENTAL INCOME	____________
STOCK/BOND PROCEEDS	____________
MISCELLANEOUS INCOME	____________
TOTAL MONTHLY INCOME	**$ ____________**

FIXED (Stationary) EXPENDITURES	Current Amount Due	Actual Payment
MORTGAGE/RENT	$ ________	$ ________
FUEL (Heating Oil, Gas, Electricity)	________	________
ELECTRICITY (No Heating)	________	________
WATER/SEWAGE	________	________
TELEPHONE	________	________
PERS. PROPERTY TAXES	________	________
AUTO LOAN, #1	________	________
AUTO LOAN, #2	________	________
AUTO INSURANCE PREMIUM	________	________
LIFE INSURANCE PREMIUM	________	________
MEDICAL/DISABILITY INSURANCE PREM.	________	________
HOMEOWNER'S INSURANCE PREMIUM	________	________
CREDIT CARD ____________	________	________
CREDIT CARD ____________	________	________
OTHER INSTALLMENT PAYMENTS	________	________
TOTAL FIXED EXPENSES	**$ ________**	**$ ________**
FLEXIBLE (Changeable) EXPENDITURES		
DONATIONS, TITHES, OFFERINGS	$ ________	$ ________
GROCERIES/BEVERAGES	________	________
BEAUTICIAN, BARBER, COSMETICS, etc.	________	________
CLOTHING	________	________
LAUNDRY/CLEANING	________	________
GASOLINE/AUTO MAINTENANCE	________	________
COMMUTE (Bus, Subway, Taxi, etc.)	________	________
ENTERTAINMENT (Restaurants, Theater, etc.)	________	________
TRAVEL/VACATION	________	________
MEDICAL COPAYS/PRESCRIPTIONS	________	________
CHILD CARE	________	________
INVESTMENTS/SAVINGS	________	________
PERSONAL ALLOWANCE	________	________
MISCELLANEOUS	________	________
TOTAL FLEXIBLE EXPENSES	**$ ________**	**$ ________**
COMBINED TOTAL EXPENDITURES	**$ ________**	**$ ________**

MY DAILY LOG OF GRACE

I will write any significant comment that involves ME on each day. At six months' intervals, I will review this entire month to discover my spiritual and financial growth experiences.

NOV.,20 ______	DAILY ENTRY * BENEFIT * BLESSING
DAY 1	______
2	______
3	______
4	______
5	______
6	______
7	______
8	______
9	______
10	______
11	______
12	______
13	______
14	______
15	______
16	______
17	______
18	______
19	______
20	______
21	______
22	______
23	______
24	______
25	______
26	______
27	______
28	______
29	______
30	______
31	______

MONTHLY CASH FLOW WORKSHEET December, 20_______

INCOME SOURCES	(Total All MONTHLY Net or 'Take Home' Amounts.)
SALARY (from current PRIMARY employment)	$ __________
PART TIME JOB Earnings	__________
SOCIAL SECURITY/PENSION	__________
CHILD SUPPORT INCOME/ALIMOMY INCOME	__________
TRUST FUND INCOME	__________
RENTAL INCOME	__________
STOCK/BOND PROCEEDS	__________
MISCELLANEOUS INCOME	__________
TOTAL MONTHLY INCOME	**$ __________**

FIXED (Stationary) **EXPENDITURES**	**Current Amount Due**	**Actual Payment**
MORTGAGE/RENT	$ __________	$ __________
FUEL (Heating Oil, Gas, Electricity)	__________	__________
ELECTRICITY (No Heating)	__________	__________
WATER/SEWAGE	__________	__________
TELEPHONE	__________	__________
PERS. PROPERTY TAXES	__________	__________
AUTO LOAN, #1	__________	__________
AUTO LOAN, #2	__________	__________
AUTO INSURANCE PREMIUM	__________	__________
LIFE INSURANCE PREMIUM	__________	__________
MEDICAL/DISABILITY INSURANCE PREM.	__________	__________
HOMEOWNER'S INSURANCE PREMIUM	__________	__________
CREDIT CARD __________	__________	__________
CREDIT CARD __________	__________	__________
OTHER INSTALLMENT PAYMENTS	__________	__________
TOTAL FIXED EXPENSES	**$ __________**	**$ __________**
FLEXIBLE (Changeable) **EXPENDITURES**		
DONATIONS, TITHES, OFFERINGS	$ __________	$ __________
GROCERIES/BEVERAGES	__________	__________
BEAUTICIAN, BARBER, COSMETICS, etc.	__________	__________
CLOTHING	__________	__________
LAUNDRY/CLEANING	__________	__________
GASOLINE/AUTO MAINTENANCE	__________	__________
COMMUTE (Bus, Subway, Taxi, etc.)	__________	__________
ENTERTAINMENT (Restaurants, Theater, etc.)	__________	__________
TRAVEL/VACATION	__________	__________
MEDICAL COPAYS/PRESCRIPTIONS	__________	__________
CHILD CARE	__________	__________
INVESTMENTS/SAVINGS	__________	__________
PERSONAL ALLOWANCE	__________	__________
MISCELLANEOUS	__________	__________
TOTAL FLEXIBLE EXPENSES	**$ __________**	**$ __________**
COMBINED TOTAL EXPENDITURES	**$ __________**	**$ __________**

MY DAILY LOG OF GRACE

I will write any significant comment that involves ME on each day. At six months' intervals, I will review this entire month to discover my spiritual and financial growth experiences.

DEC., 20 ______ DAILY ENTRY * BENEFIT * BLESSING

DAY 1 ______
2 ______
3 ______
4 ______
5 ______
6 ______
7 ______

8 ______
9 ______
10 ______
11 ______
12 ______
13 ______
14 ______

15 ______
16 ______
17 ______
18 ______
19 ______
20 ______
21 ______

22 ______
23 ______
24 ______
25 ______
26 ______
27 ______

28 ______
29 ______
30 ______
31 ______

The FOURTH Chapter

MY 'THINK, WRITE & DO' PLAN

Each month I should review, insert and implement the actions that I have written on this plan to assure a workable balanced, well-rounded schedule. These life choices are designed to make me happy and productive at helping others enjoy living a life of JOY and thanksgiving.

SAVING **A MINIMUM AMOUNT TO ACCUMULATE within the next three to seven years**

SAVINGS ACCOUNT $_________ INVESTMENTS $__________

HOW? My ways for continuous monetary growth are listed below.

1. ______________________ 1. ______________________

2. ______________________ 2. ______________________

3. ______________________ 3. ______________________

GIVING **MY CONSISTENT MONETARY GIFT and other tangible donations to charity**

CHURCH, MINISTRY or NON PROFIT GROUP		FREQUENCY OF GIFTS			
		Weekly	Monthly	Quarterly	Annually
* Tithe (10% min. and more)	$_____	______	______	______	_____
* Offering (1% up to 9%)	$_____	______	______	______	_____
Other (Clothing, Toys, Food, Furniture, Time/Volunteering, etc.)		______	______	______	_____

- IMPORTANT NOTES: Contrary to most traditional teachings on tithing and giving, I have discovered from training, studying various interpretations of the Holy Bible and related resource materials, as well as, from personal experience, the following truths:

1. The Bible (several versions) does not suggest or state in the New Testament that the 'Tithe' is to be based on gross income. (One can not donate a percentage of money that has already been deducted from total earnings.)

2. Based on repeated evidences from having a strong FAITH in GOD, I believe we need to STOP PREACHING TITHING and to START TEACHING LOVE and eternal life through the Holy Spirit. Some church leaders and teachers (similar to the Pharisees), hinder the growth of others because the whole truth is not taught. This results in confusion and financial bondage for the Christian who is trying to live according to the Word of God. We are not to give out of obligation according to any law, but out of our love for God. By His Grace, we are blessed, for God looks at our hearts and our minds. Do we give a tithe for outward show and praise from our fellowman? Are not our leaders suppose to also have *FAITH* that God will provide for them, too?

3. We are responsible for taking care of our basic needs and giving according to our ability. Let's return to the fixed expenses on the budget sheet. Some people can easily donate a tithe of ten percent; others have to strive to reach this level of giving. Their prayer and goal, in most instances, is to freely tithe. A plan, directed by God and implemented by an anointed, trained teacher can assist one in accomplishing the goals of tithing and eradicating all debt. During this process they are expected to consistently give offerings to God's Kingdom. Minimum, one tenth, givers should increase their percentages, as they are able.

   I suggest reading ALL of the Scriptures listed below. There are others related to this topic; however, this will help to document and add a clearer understanding of how to become a '*cheerful giver.*'

<u>READ FOR CLARITY AND UNDERSTANDING</u>

II Corinthians 8:7-12	Luke 11:42	Hebrews 7:17	Matthew 23:23-28
II Corinthians 9:6-8	Hebrews 8:7-13	I Corinthians 16:2	Proverbs 6:1-11

KJV - NIV - NLT - NKJV

SHARING — REGULAR ACTIVITIES AND SERVICES for and with others

LENDING MY TIME, TALENT AND CARE FOR OTHER PEOPLE (examples)

[ ] Assist at a nursing home, soup kitchen, shelter or school.

[ ] Take seasoned adults (65 plus) to the theater, dinner, the park, car rides in the country, deliver a home cooked meal to a shut-in person, etc.

[ ] Do shopping or take someone shopping who does not have transportation.

[ ] Send home made cards or telephone people to pray and express your concern.

SPECIAL REWARDS FOR MYSELF AND/OR FAMILY

[ ] Buy one special gift for myself.

[ ] Plan and implement one selected activity with family or friends

[ ] Get rest and relaxation (one day; three days; one week)

[ ] Other ____

The FIFTH Chapter

SUGGESTIONS WHEN...

I NEED MORE MONEY!

Remember the budget? The first thing I recommend is to carefully look at my budget and determine sections or items that can be deleted or reduced. If this exercise does not give me the additional cash flow that I need, I will really begin to work by examining or implementing the following actions.

1. Make a list of all my assets or use a professionally printed balance sheet.

   (See rear of book for directions on ordering various forms.)

2. Make a list of everything that I owe.

NOTE: For both items, use total amounts for the value of things that I own and for all balances that I owe. Some categories to consider are listed below:

What I OWN	**Est. Amt.**	**What I OWE**	**Est. Amt.**
Home (Real Estate)	$ ______	Mortgage	$ ______
Auto	______	Auto Loan	______
Clothing/Jewelry	______	Home Improvement Loan	______
Antiques/Collectibles	______	Education Loan	______
Household Furnishings	______	Credit Card(s)	______
Stocks/Bonds	______	Federal/State Taxes	______
Other Investments	______	Other Taxes	______
Life Insurance/Annuities	______	Charge Accounts	______
Vested Pension Benefits	______	Insurance Premiums	______
IRA/KEOGH	______	Utilities	______
Checking Account	______	Rent (one year or less)	______
Savings Account	______	Other Installment Debts	______
Cash Value/Life Insurance	______	Personal/Individual Debts	______
Miscellaneous	______	Miscellaneous	______
TOTAL	**$** ______	**TOTAL**	**$** ______

There may be other items that can be added to the above list. If so, I will include them.

Now to subtract the total amount of what I owe from what I own will equal my *total net worth.* This allows me to analyze my financial picture and decide if I should liquidate one or a few assets. I may decide to redirect some cash on hand or I may have enough personal property (good things that we do not use) to have a yard/garage sale. The use of the classified section in the local newspaper may be the best method for some other possessions. One or no more than two of the above considerations should be used to accomplish my monetary need without jeopardizing my overall financial goals.

I WANT TO WORK MY OWN HOURS

Most of the time, people will utter the above words when they are tired of the 'rat race, the office politics, the long commute, and/or the need to spend more time with the children.' A major factor derived from an honest assessment is the dislike for the current job. This justifies 'working for myself' so that I can work my own hours. Doesn't it? Having been self-employed for many years, I will briefly highlight some experiences and reflect on the knowledge that I acquired as I learned how to make an income 'my way.' The order that I am suggesting may or may not be suitable for someone else, but it is mine. Perhaps, this will prevent others from reinventing the wheel.

1. Let's look at my monthly budget, again. We will now add the total of three to six months' budget to an estimated amount for medical bills and miscellaneous expenses, in order to have this much money in the checking account BEFORE leaving the job.

   Example: Monthly Combined Total Expenditures is $3,125.00 X 3 months = $9,375.00 PLUS three months of estimated medical and miscellaneous expenses @ $900.00 = $10,275.00 of 'worry-free' planning and marketing time.

To be candid, I did not have enough money in my checking account to cover three months of living expenses. I did not abruptly leave my job, but I lacked a full understanding of the complexity involved in establishing my worth to the chaotic, competitive business arena. So, my second suggestion should have been my primary one.

2. I strongly recommend prayer and meditation for direction. Ask God to give you guidance with this challenge that you sincerely feel is the best option for you and your family. During this period, I would concentrate on the following key components in this process.

    a. **Discipline**—can I work 7-8 hours per day for four days a week or if you prefer, 5 hours per day for five days a week?
    b. **Commitment**—am I totally willing to ignore the criticism from friends or family members who think that I am mentally unbalanced?

c. **Faith (Confidence)** - am I secure in my choice to work my own hours? Is my faith in God, the evidence of my truthful spirit, combined with using my God-given talents to obtain and succeed at this task? Am I tough enough to handle the frustrations?

d. **Environment** - will I feel FREE as I work at home, from my auto or even from my garage? Will my efforts allow me to interact with people who are involved in a field or industry that is fun or enjoyable to me? NOTE: One's livelihood MUST be a natural, spontaneous ability for a truly mutually shared result to occur.

Joy, success for some people, or living a good life, God's Way, equals doing what He has ordained us to do from birth. Search for it by assessing your own innate, ingenuous, skills and talents. If you can select work that will allow you to work from home, it is the most desired. There is little or no overhead costs. I learned that it is better to stay away from loans and in some instances, grant funds. The paperwork and time that it takes to become approved, if ever, can result in a total loss. The familiar cliché, find a need and supply it, really works. Do work for a company that needs your abilities and is willing to pay you a flat amount or a percentage. This is a mutual benefit that allows the company to provide a service or a product without establishing it inside the firm.

The primary home office or business does not dictate high startup costs. I suggest the following methods. Read before implementing because the order may slightly vary for you.

1. Search newspaper classified ads for used office furniture (desk, chair, table and file cabinet). Some items can be bought for a few dollars and some can be acquired free.
2. Get a separate telephone line, computer equipment, a used, but good typewriter and a fax machine. Find inexpensive software equipment. If you need to learn how to operate the computer, check with your local library for free classes. Otherwise, find a friend who can give you basic instructions.
3. Have brochures and letterhead/envelopes printed. Think carefully about your business and how you want to present it to the public. Ask for help if this area is not within your abilities. Do

black and white printing until you begin to make money and can afford stationery in two or three colors. Business cards are usually the first thing that a person will use for advertising. Think! You cannot and should not try to sell your business on a calling card. A brochure is a more effective way to communicate your services, your locale and telephone number.

4. Do research by visiting county offices to determine if your home is in a proper zoning area. Determine the type of business organization you want to establish (a sole proprietorship, a partnership, or a corporation). Will you need a license or some other type of certification? Most importantly, decide to do this part time to test your idea and the target market. A feasibility study is always helpful; you can do this yourself by meeting with people who are in the field and asking for advice about the best way to handle the task. Do not spend all your startup money on consultants, if you can do these functions yourself. Otherwise, make an attempt to barter with a professional for what you need.

Keep an open mind for learning. ASK FOR HELP from people who know. Do not be afraid to call or contact someone who has been in a related business that can offer you assistance. In the rear of this book, call, email or mail the form to get information about attending one or more of the workshops, conferences or retreats that are given each year. These sessions provide you with verbal and written materials that are helpful for your personal and business budgets.

TAKE CONTROL; YOU HAVE THE POWER!

"And you shall remember the Lord your God, for it is He who gives you power to get wealth, that
***He may establish His covenant which He swore to your fathers, as it is this day."*...NKJV Deut. 8:18**

I WANT TO INCREASE AND STABILIZE MY FINANCES

NO WORK...> NO MONEY...equals...> NO INVESTMENTS. It takes money to buy investment products. It takes investments to earn more income. Briefly, I want to suggest methods and vehicles that can be used to build a strong financial base.

a. DO NOT use unnecessary energy. Make a weekly plan of things to do.

b. Know what you want to do and do not allow criticisms from others to deter you.

c. Recognize that opportunity does not usually knock twice; be ready to accept it and immediately act on it.

d. Be responsible for your actions and learn from your mistakes. There is no time for pity parties. When you fall or fail, take a few hours or a day to rest. Then, regroup by writing what you perceive as the causes for the temporary delay, followed by new approaches to implement. Write what you learned.

To make extra income, I engaged in all of the money-making possibilities (at various times) listed below. During a period of about fifteen to eighteen years, I made enough money to take care of my personal budget and save (modest amounts) for investment purposes.

1. CREATED A JOB BY ASKING FOR WORK—based on my interests and goals.
2. USED THE COMPUTER—wrote promotional pieces for other small businesses
3. CREATED AND/OR PRODUCED PRODUCTS—designed and produced heart shaped name tags; made and sold sweet potato pies, and notepads.
4. MET WEALTHY PEOPLE—Became a personal assistant to a disabled one
5. VOLUNTEERED WITH NON-PROFIT GROUPS—Earned a small stipend from one and received food donations from another
6. PLANNED ENTERTAINMENT OUTINGS FOR SINGLE OLDER PEOPLE—Made all arrangements, provided transportation and received complimentary theatre ticket and dinner from the group

7. BOUGHT HOME AND RENTED SPACE—rented three bedrooms to professional people who also had access to kitchen privileges. Rent received was equivalent to my mortgage payment.
8. HAD PERIODIC YARD SALES—Obtained donations from friends and used own personal property for yard sales; advertised in local newspapers.

As I continued to learn more and more about creating an investment portfolio, I developed a plan for investing and increasing my net worth. Listed below are some of the key steps that I formulated. It took and still takes consistent efforts to make my plan materialize into a stable financial base.

1. YOU CAN OBTAIN INVESTMENT DOLLARS BY:
   a. Saving the same minimum amount EVERY month. Have the attitude that savings is as essential as 'drinking a glass of water'.
   b. Stop buying without a plan; in short, no 'spur of the moment' purchases.
   c. Searching for discounts and special sales; buying good, used items.

1. YOU CAN OBTAIN INVESTMENT DOLLARS BY (continued):

    d. Using only ONE credit card with a low interest rate.

    e. Refinancing mortgage loans or consolidating debt at the lowest, 'qualifiable' rate.

    f. Buying or retaining one whole life or universal life insurance policy on both spouses to cover estate taxes and cost of living when one of them leaves earth for heaven. Make certain, the face amount remains and the premium decreases or is constant throughout the life of the policyholder.

    g. Researching several auto insurance companies to get the best rate for required coverage.

    h. Paying less taxes (a CPA or tax accountant is worth the fee). Complete the reservation form in the rear and learn the rationale at one of our family budget workshops.

    i. Decreasing WEIGHT by ignoring 'fast food' establishments. Save and plan for one or two monthly 'fine dining' engagements. Make your own lunch for work. **NOTE: $5.00 per day for lunch = $1,200.00 minimum per year**

2. YOU SHOULD STICK TO YOUR BUDGET, except to increase savings and charitable donations after depleting a debt.
3. YOU NEED TO CAREFULLY DIVERSIFY your investment portfolio. Because interest rates rise and fall, the order of purchasing the suggested vehicles becomes a personal choice based on the current market trends.

    a. Personal Savings Account (this is NOT an investment BUT a necessity).
    b. Mutual Stock Funds
    c. Mutual Bond Funds
    d. Mutual Stock & Bond Funds
    e. Personal Real Estate
    f. Treasury Bonds; Series EE; I; HH Savings Bonds) or Treasury Securities
    g. CD's (Certificates of Deposit)
    h. International/Global Funds
    i. Investment Real Estate
    j. Home Based Business

A few passing thoughts based on my personal growth experiences are: 1) You can not accumulate money by working for someone else; 2) Your investments should be making money while you are sleeping; and 3) You should have dividend checks (two or more) arriving in the mail each month, along with a decent sum that is derived from your part time home business. Build or implement your plan to satisfy the above three major accomplishments and spend more time (with dollars and deeds) assisting your brothers or neighbors who are less fortunate. This; my friend, is one of the utmost ways of living the 'GOOD LIFE, GOD'S WAY'.

LOVING OTHERS

The second greatest commandment is:

"Love Your Neighbor As Yourself."

...NLT Matt. 22:39

SERVING OTHERS

A real leader serves others. If there is something
that needs to be done, do it as a faithful servant.

... NLT Matt. 21:25-28

LOVING GOD

You must love the Lord your God with all your heart, all your soul and all your mind. This is the First and Greatest Commandment...NLT Matt. 22:37-38

The SIXTH Chapter

THE PEOPLE SPEAK

LETTERS AND WORKSHOP EVALUATIONS have been received from many individuals who have attended our workshops, conferences and/or retreats for more than twenty-three (23) years. We have taken a sample from slightly more than one thousand (1,000) of these precious feedback communication pieces to share with you. The GOOD NEWS of this ministry is spread by 'word of mouth.' Participants have come from various cities throughout the United States and as far away as, Africa (Ghana and Kenya) to date. However, in memory of my mother, who made her transition to Heaven on February 15, 2001, I must tell you that she rejected my ministry in the beginning. Her lack of understanding and my not doing the 'traditional' things that women usually do in the church, did not fit into the norm. BUT, after she had traveled with me to an evangelistic conference at Southern Seminary in Louisville, Kentucky and following her attendance at a handful of our annual budget retreats and workshops, she wrote the following comments on the evaluation form, dated June 5, 1999. On February 13, 2001, her last instructions to me were: "Keep the Ministry going; get back to your singing; and take care of Duchess (our family pet)."

> "The most beneficial part of this workshop was what I learned about how we are to tithe to the Lord. I pray that the Lord will continue to bless my daughter, L.A., to do a great mission for Him through this budget ministry."
>
> Rose (Tucker) Hicks
> Chattanooga, TN

Let us not forget that many people do not complete the evaluation forms. We further believe personal finance or money remains secretive. Regardless of one's socioeconomic status, we learn; we share; and our personal finances remain closed. Enjoy reading the few responses that we have selected, if you please?

Letters and Workshop Evaluations (continued)

FROM: 1979 **TO: 2002**

"The presenter seem to be well informed about her subject matter."
Catherine Blackmon
Washington, D. C.

"I really enjoyed the class. It has shown me how to count my blessings in reference to my finances. I also have a better understanding of tithes and offerings..."
Alice Swann
Georgia

Dear Ms. L.A.:

Enclosed is a dollar for the Father, one for the Son and another for the Holy Spirit..."
Marline Coughman
Washington, D. C.

Dear Mrs. L. A. Smith:

I want to take this opportunity to thank you again for presenting our students with information regarding financial solvency, preparing a financial plan and the benefits of entrepreneurship...I wish that they would have the same enthusiastic response to all of our lectures. I am hopeful that you will return as a guest lecturer on a regular basis..."

A. K. Wutoh, Ph.D., R.Ph.
Assistant Professor/Howard University

Dear L. A. Smith:

"The words, "Thank You," don't seem adequate to express our appreciation for all you have done for us. Not only did you help us overcome a difficult financial situation; you equipped us with financial and spiritual knowledge that we so desperately needed..."

Matthew & Debra Rodgers
Lithonia, GA

Dear L. A.:

Although I am not at the conference, in person, I am there in spirit. Please accept this donation as an expression of my continuous support and admiration for your ministry. The Lord's blessings to you.

Greg Mayfield
Wheaton, MD

"I appreciate the workshop very much.

...I am going to apply what I gained and

get down to basic training right away.

Thank you, L. A."

Myrtice Ackey
Decatur, GA

"Ms. L. A. Smith was excellent in her
presentation; very knowledgeable;
provided a lot of valuable information;
very personable and gave us time for
questions and answers."

Mary B. DeaVone
Hyattsville, MD

TO: Evangelist L. A.:

My personal experience as a participant at the Fund Raising for Evangelism Conference during 23-27 May, 2001 has greatly blessed me. I am beginning to expand my coast, boundary and territory due to the exposition of insights of fund raising for evangelism for the disabled, orphans and HIV/AIDS children. Furthermore, it is helping me to reorganize my ministry for the betterment.

Rev. Dr. F. A. Kwesi Biney
Executive Director & Pastor
Mount Horeb Glory Ministries
Sunyani, GHANA, Africa

Dear L. A.:

"It is always a wonderful pleasure speaking to you. I really look forward to the conference...Thank you so much for your warm heart..."

Minh Pham, Speaker/Consultant
Greenbelt, MD

"I really enjoyed the seminar because I learned a lot about budgeting money and investing."

Mildred Hicks
Chattanooga, TN

"As usual, L. A., you make me more aware of how to manage in every way. Thank you."

Susan Hewan
Silver Spring, MD

Dear Evangelist L. A. Smith:

The Trustee Board and attendees at the two part workshop (Cash In On The Benefits/Blessings) are just overjoyed with the after effect of your presentations. We are still beaming with the information received and motivated to act.

You captivated the group with your ability to blend the spiritual truth and humor...We offer you our thanks and prayers for your continued success in your future presentations. May God give you added strength to stand where HE has placed you.

Edna J. Harris
Trustee Chairperson
Faith Community Baptist Church
Silver Spring, MD

Dear Evangelist:

Praise the Lord. I have come across information about your FUND RAISING FOR EVANGELISM CONFERENCE. I am a pastor of a growing church here in Nairobi and I am sure the conference will be beneficial to me and our church...

Rev. Obed Ochwanyi
Senior Pastor & Director
Church of God/Buruburu Comm. Centre
Nairobi, KENYA, E. Africa

"This is the BEST financial/budgeting workshop I have attended. L. A. covers a wide spectrum of topics on budgeting and investing without going over the participants' head."

Charlotte Payne, P.A.
Laurel, MD

"Thank you for letting me feel so special at the Prayer and Recognition Luncheon. It was a very inspiring occasion."

Patricia Allen, RN
Clinton, MD

Evangelist L. A. Smith:

Greetings in the name of our Lord, Jesus Christ. God has been so faithful to us since I came from America. You gave me the financial audio tapes from your radio program and they have been a blessing to the servants of the Lord, here in Nairobi. Some members have shown an interest in coming for the budget training.

Now, I can share in my knowledge of finances and have been called to various churches to share about budgeting money. What a miracle! I have achieved all of this because of you, L. A. Smith and your ministry. God Bless You.

Rev. Andrew Okusi Eyenga
Nairobi, KENYA, E. Africa

"L. A. Smith was very informative and motivational. She allowed me to see how much I need to 'get my house in order,' financially. Thank you; I look forward to another class."

Leary Brock
Washington, D.C.

"The workshop was very good. I appreciated the handouts on the growth steps in the Master Life Plan."

Janet Gibbs
Beltsville, MD

Dear L. A.:

Please know that my prayers are with you during this exciting time when you and Edward travel to the Amsterdam 2000 Conference. I am sure you will have words of wisdom for other evangelists and ministers.

George Blackmon
Washington, D. C.

Dear Ms. Smith:

...Thank you so much for designing a budget for me. You have truly been a blessing and you have brought things to my attention about my finances that I never would have considered...In the past, I had applied for a consolidation loan and was denied twice.

By quoting Scripture, you informed me that I am to be a lender, not a borrower and that the time has come for me to become more responsible in handling my finances. After our meeting, I followed your advice. First, I prayed to God and told Him that I put it all in His hands...If I was denied again for a loan, I asked God to give me the ways and means to double up on my payments. Second, I contacted my credit union and requested the loan, again. I even asked for the person who handles appeals, in the event my application was denied.

The loan officer contacted me the next day and told me I was approved. The following day, the checks arrived via Federal Express. I was floored; I could not believe everything worked out...

Because of God and you, I feel like a ton of bricks have been lifted from my shoulders. You have made me aware of what I have been doing wrong over the years. I also appreciate the time given to explain a true budget to me and the way you used Bible Scriptures to support your statements. The budget you prepared helps me to use my money wisely, while allowing me to have a weekly allowance to do the things I enjoy, in moderation.

Again, thank you for giving me the encouragement to remember that through faith, all things are possible. I will be sending email messages to friends and coworkers to advise that they attend one of your seminars to become better informed about debt management and effective budgeting.

Donna D. Bailey
Maryland

"...I will close this letter with prayer.
Dear God; In the name of Jesus, I thank you for allowing me to attend and participate at the Family Budget Retreat. I was so blessed and so honored to do what you asked me to do. I learned so much and I was an asset, as well...I ask your special blessings upon L.A. and Mr. Roberts. I also ask that you continue to provide and bless the entire ministry, financially, spiritually, and in every other way. I thank you for all things, in the name of Jesus. Amen."

Inez Watson and Family
Ft. Meade, MD

The SEVENTH Chapter

TAKE A BREAK!

SCRAMBLE/SCRAMBLE PUZZLES

RELAX YOUR MIND. Unscramble these letters; write only one letter to a space. Unscramble the words; form a complete thought. The messages may give you important directions or guidance.

1. ___ ___	ETSB
___ ___ ___	EB
___ ___ ___ ___	THE
___ ___	STBE
___ ___ ___	FO
___ ___ ___ ___	EHT

2. ___ ___ ___ ___ ___ ___ ___ ___	DNA
___ ___ ___ ___ ___ ___ ___	SCECSUS
___ ___ ___	IASOCTN
___ ___ ___ ___ ___ ___ ___ ___ ___ ___	ETSVPIIO
___ ___ ___ ___ ___ ___ ___ ___	TEMIDENRE
___ ___ ___ ___ ___ ___	YSSTPECEINR

3. ___ ___ ___ ___

___ ___ ___ ___ ___ ___ ___

___ ___ ___ ___ ___ ___

___ ___ ___ ___

URDANO
PSOT
DDAE
LWGKIAN

4. ___ ___ ___ ___

___ ___ ___ ___ ___ ___ ___ ___ ___

___ ___ ___ ___

___ ___ ___

___ ___ ___ ___ ___ ___

___ ___ ___ ___ ___

___ ___ ___

___ ___ ___

OTPFRI
YPA
DUCLO
UROY
LNPA
SHHLUEODO
ORF
FOF

5. ___ ___ ___ ___ ___ ___ ___ ___ ___

___ ___

___ ___ ___ ___ ___ ___ ___ ___ ___

___ ___ ___

___ ___ ___ ___ ___ ___ ___ ___ ___

___ ___ ___ ___ ___ ___

___ ___ ___ ___ ___ ___

VESLLE
HHRIGE
SI
EGVCHAIHNI
RESCEYANS
ORF
RDNEEAUNC

6. ___ ___ ___

___ ___ ___ ___ ___ ___

___

___ ___ ___ ___ ___ ___

___ ___

___ ___ ___ ___ ___

TA
AEEMCB
RBHIT
A
NREIWN
UOY

7. ___ ___ ___ ___

___ ___ ___ ___ ___

___ ___ ___ ___ ___ ___ ___

___ ___

___ ___ ___ ___ ___ ___

___ ___ ___ ___ ___ ___ ___ ___

___ ___ ___ ___ ___ ___

VPEISIOT
NTOD
BRABSO
NYREEG
OT
PGSOESN
LWAOL

<u>OUR DAILY LIVES SHOULD INCLUDE LEARNING.</u>

"A wise person is hungry for truth, while the fool feeds on trash...If you reject criticism, you only harm yourself; but if you listen to correction, you grow in understanding." **...NLT Proverbs 15:14, 32**

8. ___ ___ ___ ___ ULAESQ
LSFE

___ ___ ___ ___ ___ ___ ___ ___ ___ ___ ___

___ ___ ___ ___ ___ PPEHINSAS
TFSSAITNIOAC

___ ___ ___ ___ ___ ___ ___ ___ ___

9. ___ ___ ___ ___ ___ ___ WRRAED
NHKTA

___ ___ ___ ___ ___ UYO
SMTO

___ ___ ___ LIWL
OUY

___ ___ ___ ___ IAGYSN

___ ___ ___ ___ ___ ___

___ ___ ___

___ ___ ___ ___

10. ___ ___ ___ ___ NAD
FCTOORM

___ ___ ___ APYR
YVDEAEYR

___ ___ ___ ___ ___ EEACP
RFO

___ ___ ___

___ ___ ___ ___ ___ ___ ___

___ ___ ___ ___ ___ ___ ___ ___

11. ___ ___ ___ PEHL
KAS
RFO

___ ___ ___

___ ___ ___ ___

12. ___ ___ ___ ___ ___ ___ RFO
YEDRAVEY

___ ___ ___ ___ ___ ___ ___ ___ ___ ___ ___ ___

EERACT
___ ___ ___ PSANSHEIP
TPSOIIREPUOTN

___ ___ ___ ___ ___ ___ ___ ___ ___

___ ___ ___ ___ ___ ___ ___ ___

13. ___ ___ ___ ___ ___ ___ ADDUECET
CEEBMO

___ ___ ___ ___ ___ ___ ___ ___ ___ ___

___ ___ ___ ___ ___ ___ ___ ___ LNAIFNACLIY

ALLOW GOD TO LEAD YOU.
"In his heart a man plans his course, but the Lord determines his steps" or
"We can make our plans, but the Lord determines our steps."
...NIV & NLT Proverbs 16:9

14. ___ ___ ___ ___ ___ ___

___ ___ ___

___ ___ ___ ___ ___ ___

___ ___ ___ ___ ___ ___

___ ___ ___ ___ ___ ___ ___ ___ ___

GUBTED
EHT
PROWSHSOK
DTNEAT
YMLAFI

15. ___ ___ ___ ___

___ ___ ___ ___ ___ ___

HVTIER

TESL

ANSWERS—Scramble/Scramble Puzzles

1. BE THE BEST OF THE BEST.
2. POSITIVE ACTIONS AND PERSISTENCY DETERMINE SUCCESS.
3. STOP WALKING AROUND DEAD.
4. YOUR HOUSEHOLD PLAN FOR PROFIT COULD PAY OFF.
5. ENDURANCE IS NECESSARY FOR ACHIEVING HIGHER LEVELS.
6. YOU BECAME A WINNER AT BIRTH.
7. DON'T ALLOW SPONGES TO ABSORB POSITIVE ENERGY.
8. SELF SATISFACTION EQUALS HAPPINESS.
9. SAYING THANK YOU WILL REWARD YOU MOST.
10. PRAY FOR PEACE AND COMFORT EVERYDAY.
11. ASK FOR HELP.
12. CREATE OPPORTUNITIES FOR HAPPINESS EVERYDAY.
13. BECOME FINANCIALLY EDUCATED.
14. ATTEND THE FAMILY BUDGET WORKSHOPS.
15. LET'S THRIVE!

*NOTE: For **more Scramble/Scramble Puzzles**, please complete the enclosed Order/Registration Form.*

REFERENCES

Of

THE HOLY BIBLE

NLT	The New Life Translation (Life Application Study Bible), 1996
NIV	The New International Version, 1999, 1984
NLT	The New Living Translation, 1996
KJV	The King James Version (Dictionary Concordance), 1977
NKJV	The New King James Version (Old & New Testaments), 1994

SUGGESTED READINGS

A BETTER WAY TO LIVE, Mandino, Og, Bantam Books, New York, 1990

PEACE WITH GOD, Graham, Billy (Special Crusade Edition) Worldwide Publications' Minneapolis, MN, 1984

WHO MOVED MY CHEESE? Johnson, Spencer, M.D., Putnam's Sons Publishers, NY, 1998

THE RIGHT WAY TO INVEST IN MUTUAL FUNDS, Updegrave, Walter, Money Book Club, Warner Books, Inc., NY, 1996

GUIDE TO UNDERSTANDING PERSONAL FINANCE, Wall Street Journal, Morris and Siegel, Lightbulb Press, 1992, '93, '94, etc.

EVERYTHING YOU NEED TO KNOW ABOUT MONEY AND INVESTING, Fisher & Turkington, Prentice Hall Press, NJ, 1999

PROSPERITY ON GOD'S TERMS, Price, Frederick K. C., Harrison House, Oklahoma, 1990

TITHING IS A MATTER OF LOVE...NOT LAW, Jakes, T.D., Sr., Dallas, TX, 1997

MORE WEALTH WITHOUT RISK, Givens, Charles, Simon & Schuster, NY, 1991

TONGUE FU!, Horn, Sam, St. Martin's Press, NY, 1996

QUICK TO LISTEN, SLOW TO SPEAK, Fisher, Robert E., Tyndale House Publishers, IL, 1987

MEN, WOMEN, AND RELATIONSHIPS, Gray, John, Ph.D., Beyond Words Publishing, OR, 1993

SUCCESS MOTIVATION THRU THE WORD, Capps, Charles, Harrison House, OK, 1982

MAKES ME WANT TO HOLLER, McCall, Nathan, Random House, NY, 1994

GOD'S STORY (Finding Meaning For Your Life Through Knowing God), Lotz, Anne Graham, Word Publishing, TN, 1999

WHAT EVERY RELIGION NEEDS TO KNOW ABOUT THE GODHEAD, Finch, Larry, Sr., Ph.D., Brentwood Christian Press, GA, 2000

THE BLACK THREAD, Pledger, Marian E., Wholeness Publications, Canton, OH, 1998

BEEP! BEEP! Bell, Chip R., and Harari, Oren, Warner Books, NY, 2000.

APPENDICES

Annual Schedule Financial Management (Stewardship)Training

MANAGING YOUR INCOME, GOD'S WAY

Good News & Give Aways, Inc.
FAMILY BUDGET WORKSHOPS
P.O. Box 929, Gainesville, VA 20156
1-877-951-3474 (Toll Free)

www.LA-speaks.net Email: Goodnews23@aol.com

PLAN EARLY (Preferably 45-90 days in advance) CALL US

May (the third or fourth Saturday) **PRAYER & RECOGNITION LUNCHEON** ... Bring someone special and honor them. Everyone is saluted with praise and gifts at this event.

October (the fourth Saturday; Sunday is sometimes included) **FAMILY BUDGET BUSINESS FAIR**. This annual event allows nonprofits, small businessess and community groups to display or exhibit their products or services. Everyone learns how to more effectively manage their monies at home and/ or in the work environment. Many ideas are shared for getting rid of debt and making money without a job.

Other Dates You may inquire about having one of the above events, a conference, or family reunion at **YOUR LOCATION**.

Check our **HOST A FREE WORKSHOP** program, online at www.LA-speaks.net or call us toll free at 1/877-951-3474.

Remember, we will be happy to serve you as a **SPEAKER, SEMINAR PRESENTER** and/or **SINGER** for your special occasion.

MANAGING YOUR INCOME, GOD'S WAY

Good News & Give Aways, Inc.
FAMILY BUDGET WORKSHOPS

LOCATION: Gainesville and Warrenton, in the state of Virginia is approximately 45-50 miles from Washington, D.C. Suggested hotel accomodations can be supplied upon request.

REGISTRATION FORM (Call or Email us for the registration donation and/or lodging fee.)

NAME ______________________ Today's Date __________
FULL ADDRESS ______________________________
PHONE ______________________ EMAIL ______________

Workshop Month	Workshop Title	No. Attending
____________	____________	____________
____________	____________	____________

Make CHECKS payable to:

Good News & Give Aways, Inc.
P.O. Box 929
Gainesville, VA 20156
1/877-951-3474
www.LA-speaks.net

Check Payment Method

- ☐ Online: www.LA-speaks.net
- ☐ Check/Money Order
- ☐ Western Union - Fedex/UPS Delivery

WE WILL VISIT YOUR AREA and
HELP YOU RAISE FUNDS FOR YOUR GROUP!

IMPORTANT ACTION STEP

Devote approximately two (2) hours per week to budget needs (reviewing mail, balancing check book analyzing bank statements, paying bills, etc).

Stewardship/Management

HOME **WORSHIP PLACE**

Thanks be to God for His indescribable gift. *II Corinthians 9:15*

In GIVING, be responsible to your household; share with others as you are able. **STRIVE TO TITHE!**

GRANDMA KNOWS BEST

(SUGGESTIONS)

CONVENIENCE COSTS **YOU**

Automatic/Electronic Checking Payments
ATM Transactions Check Credit Cards - Debit Cards

If you need a few extra days before a check is deposited and clears, DO NOT use electronic payment systems. Write your own check or submit a collection date that is more convenient.

Example: Most mortgage companies use the 15th of the month as their cutoff date. Send your check or arrange for it to be withdrawn from your account the 7th or 8th. This eliminates their practice of withdrawing on the first (1st) when all of your deposits have probably not been received.

Develop a workable budget and get cash for your lunches and/or any other purchases that may total ten dollars ($10.) or less during a biweekly or monthly period. Avoid unplanned purchases. SAVE the ATM fee money in the 'cookie jar.'

If you do not balance your checkbook or online banking statement, please HESITATE before using these credit/debit cards. You will find it difficult to deteremine how much money you have or how it was spent. You may be guilty of spending too much for lunch, unnecessary items (toys for the children, etc.), unbudgeted gasoline. It could amount to several hundred dollars ($400.+) per month. This money could be saved, invested or used as extra principal on your mortgage.

More than two (2) credit cards, with each balance in excess of $3,000., may be a focal point to seriously consider for elimination. Late payments, more than two within a twelve months timeframe, require a letter to the creditor. Give a legitimate reason for the delayed payments and suggest an amount that you can reasonably submit each month. Putting it in writing helps both parties. Consider closing one account to avoid other purchases as you work to payoff the owed balance. WHAT IS YOUR CREDIT SCORE? Low 350-900 High. Request your FREE Annual Credit Report .... 1-877-322-8228 www.annualcreditreport.com

Already Wealthy But a Few Sense Short!

Create your estate portfolio, whether you are single or married. The major contents should include the following items:

a) Last Will & Testament
b) Living Will (for medical purposes)
c) Power of Attorney (or Dual)
d) Insurance Policies
e) Birth Certificates
f) Marriage/Death Certificates
g) Financial Statements
h) Social Security Documents

ABOUT THE AUTHOR

Minister L. A. (as she is professionally known) is a graduate and former employee of Howard University. She has been twice listed in **Who's Who of America, Finance and Industry, 1997** and the **South and Southwest, 1995;** selected as an **Outstanding Young Woman of America**, and was inducted as a member of **Phi Beta Lambda** and **Kappa Delta Pi** honor societies.

As a business owner from 1979 to the early 1990's, she founded and managed a printing corporation, an insurance brokerage agency and a Biblical/Business training consulting firm. She gained prior work experience in the banking, mortgage and credit union industries. In 1989, she established the non profit incorporated ministry, Good News & Give Aways, Inc. Retreats and workshops in various parts of the United States and as far away as Amsterdam, The Netherlands in the year 2000 plus a weekly radio broadcast, namely, "Managing Your Income and Personal Budget," have been the major components that constitute this Higher Calling for Evangelist Smith.

Her writings and published works have included two other books, plays and numerous family budget training manuals such as: "The Most Precious Moments," "Let's Consider A Sociological View of Employment," "A Reversible Oreo," and "Making My Paycheck Grow."

In addition to other travels related to her ministry, L.A. accepted an invitation to share with other children of our Lord and Savior, Jesus Christ, in Greece during June and July, 2007. Smith-Roberts is also a licensed minister and has been the recipient of numerous awards, honors and certifications. She has surrounded her self with capable business, faith-oriented and medical consultants.

Before she became a full time teaching evangelist, she served in different capacities in her local church affilliations (church treasurer, member/trustee board, soloist and Sunday school teacher). From 2001 to early 2004, several pastors, ministers and other clergy persons traveled from Africa and U.S. locations to the newly constructed Family Budget Institute conference center in Maryland for training in budgeting, ministry development and membership growth.

To learn to live better lives, God's way, contact Minister L. A. at www.LAspeaks.net 1/877-951-3474; Email: Goodnews23@aol.com or LAspeaks@comcast.net.

******

Printed in the United States
140238LV00003B/4/P